The Little Mouse Learning Books

Little Simon

THE LITTLE MOUSE 1 2 3

Helen Craig

Text by Katharine Holabird

ZERO

0 is for zero or nothing. Nothing
could be when you have lost your
hat and you have nothing to wear

zero

on your head. Or nothing could be when you have eaten all the choco-lates and now there are none left.

ONE

Sammy Shopkeeper is weighing out one bag of sugar and there is one bee waiting for a taste. There are many single things on the table.

one

They are called single because there is only one of each shape and size.

TWO

Daniel and his daddy are a pair of little mice. A pair is two of something. There is a pair of butterflies in Daniel's book and a pair of

two

butterflies flying overhead. Daniel's daddy has two pairs of glasses. Can you find any other pairs in this picture?

THREE

Three small friends meet on a hot summer's day to eat three triple ice cream cones made up of three different flavors. Triple means

three

three of something. How many other groups of three things can you find in this picture?

FOUR

The four children of the Fieldmouse family are watching their mother wash four plates, four cups, four saucers, and four spoons. It's the

four

fourth day of the month and the small hand on the clock is pointing to four. What time do you think it is?

FIVE

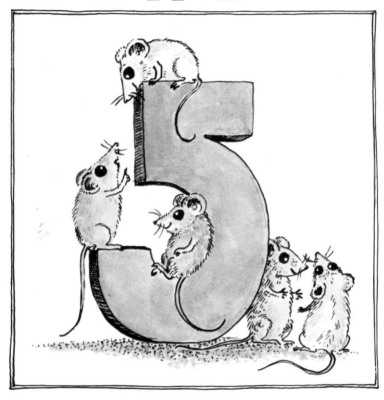

Peter Potter is making five red vases. The fifth one is still spinning on the potter's wheel. He has already made five blue vases, five

five

round jars, and five green statues.
How many pottery tools can you
count?

SIX

Six friends are playing in the garden with six pretty marbles. Three big butterflies are watching their game and three more butterflies

six

are flying away. Three plus three makes six. Matilda Mouseling is hanging out five blue aprons. Where is the sixth apron?

SEVEN

Buster and Billy Baker are putting
seven round rolls in the hot oven.
Seven large loaves are on the table,

seven

seven French loaves are in the basket, and seven crusty buns have just come out of the oven.

EIGHT

Grandpa Gardener comes to the greenhouse every day to look after eight green plants growing in eight orange pots. There are little insects

eight

who like to visit the plants too.
How many insects can you find in
the greenhouse? Do you know
what they are called?

NINE

Nine fierce wasps are flying around the sweet strawberry jam. Mother Mouse has already put nine labels

nine

on nine jars of jam to store for the wintertime. Can you find any other sets of nine in this picture?

TEN

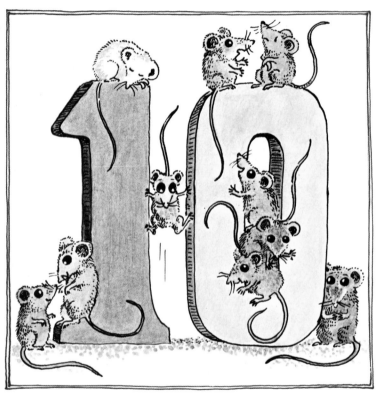

Cathy and Charles Cook are peel-
ing ten potatoes for their supper.
There are also ten black pots in the
kitchen. Seven are hanging on the

ten

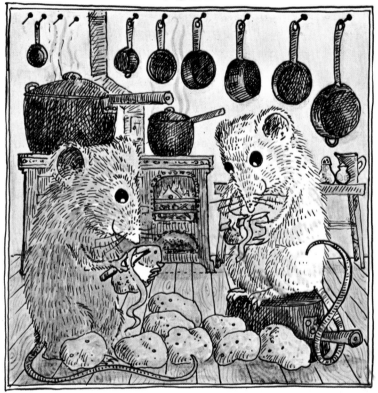

wall and two are sitting on the stove, but one is in a very strange place. Can you find it?

ELEVEN

Timothy is dropping apples into Bertha's basket. There are three apples in her basket and eight apples in the tree. That makes

eleven

eleven apples altogether. There are
also eleven trees in the orchard.
Can you count the number of rungs
on Timothy's ladder?

TWELVE

It is now twelve o'clock and twelve o'clock is midday or noon. Helen is bringing in twelve pink roses from her garden. Ben is playing with

twelve

twelve big building blocks. Each
block has a number on it. Can you
count from one to twelve?

PRINTED IN BELGIUM BY

INTERNATIONAL BOOK PRODUCTION